The Final Days

Leader Guide

The Final Days:
A Lenten Journey through the Gospels

The Final Days

978-1-7910-3416-0

978-1-7910-3417-7 eBook

The Final Days: Leader Guide

978-1-7910-3418-4

978-1-7910-3419-1 eBook

The Final Days: DVD

978-1-7910-3420-7

Also by Matt Rawle

The Faith of a Mockingbird

The Salvation of Doctor Who

Hollywood Jesus

The Redemption of Scrooge

What Makes a Hero?

The Gift of the Nutcracker

The Grace of Les Miserables

The Heart That Grew Three Sizes

Jesus Revealed

Experiencing Christmas

With Magrey R. deVega, Ingrid McIntyre, and April Casperson

Almost Christmas

For more information, visit MattRawle.com.

MATT RAWLE

The Final Days

A Lenten Journey *through the* Gospels

LEADER GUIDE

Abingdon Press | Nashville

The Final Days:

A Lenten Journey through the Gospels

Leader Guide

978-1-7910-3418-4

MANUFACTURED IN THE UNITED STATES OF AMERICA

Contents

About the Leader Guide Writer

The Rev. Michael S. Poteet is an ordained Minister of Word and Sacrament in the Presbyterian Church (U.S.A.). A graduate of the College of William and Mary and Princeton Theological Seminary, he serves the larger church as a Christian education writer, biblical storyteller, and guest preacher. You can find his occasional musings on the meetings of faith and fiction at http://www.bibliomike.com.

Introduction

In *The Final Days*, Matt Rawle (Lead Pastor, Asbury United Methodist Church, Bossier City, Louisiana) shares with readers his fascination with the fact that the Gospels all tell the story of Jesus—especially the story of his passion (his suffering and death)—from different perspectives. For Matt, observing, studying, and reflecting on the differences between Matthew, Mark, Luke, and John's accounts is no mere academic exercise, but an invitation to encounter Jesus anew, to see him through the eyes of different witnesses, and to deepen our own faith in the process.

This Leader Guide is intended to help you lead a small group of adults from your congregation in such an encounter with Jesus through Bible study. It gives you logistical pointers, Scripture readings, and study questions you can use to plan and lead six sessions, corresponding to the six chapters of Matt's book:

- Session 1—Meet You at the Flagpole gives participants a broad overview of how and why the New Testament's four Gospels tell Jesus's story differently, and looks at Matthew, Mark, and Luke's accounts of Jesus's prayer before his arrest to spark reflection on their own "passion."
- Session 2—Looking for a Messiah highlights three distinct messianic images from the Old Testament and considers how Jesus does and does not meet the expectations these

images raise in his entrance into Jerusalem. It also prompts consideration of how Jesus's death saves by reviewing three different models of the Atonement.

- Session 3—Yes, I Am: The Passion according to Mark examines how people's responses to Jesus in Mark's account of Jesus's crucifixion identify them as "insiders" or "outsiders," and asks how participants can feed a "holy imagination" to help them hear and respond to Jesus amid the "noise" of the world.
- Session 4—You Have Said So, but I Say to You: The Passion according to Matthew investigates how Matthew's narration of Jesus's ministry, and his passion, aims to move people to "ask better questions" that lead to right relationships with God and with other people.
- Session 5—A New Covenant to Remember: The Passion according to Luke spotlights the fast pace of Luke's Passion narrative, paying special attention to what and who Jesus takes time to remember, and what implications Jesus's remembrance has for his followers today.
- Session 6—A Word that Weeps: The Passion according to John focuses on the Passion from the high, cosmic vantage point of the Fourth Gospel, and how power and truth look different from that perspective.

Although this Leader Guide is written with the assumption that both leaders and participants will also be reading *The Final Days*, its quotations from Matt's book and its direct references to Scripture mean it can also be used on its own.

Each session contains the following elements to draw from as you plan six in-person, virtual, or hybrid sessions:

- Session Objectives
- Biblical Foundations—Scripture texts for the session, in the New Revised Standard Version, Updated Edition.

- Before Your Session—Tips to help you prepare a productive session.
- Starting Your Session—Discussion questions intended to "warm up" your group for fruitful discussion.
- Book Discussion Questions—You likely will not be able or want to use all the questions in every session, so feel free to pick and choose based on your group's interests and the Spirit's leading.
- Closing Your Session—A focused discussion or reflection, often suggesting action to take beyond the session.
- Opening and Closing Prayers

Thank you for your willingness to lead! May you and your group find your study of *The Final Days* an interesting, exciting, and enriching encounter with God's Word.

Session 1
Meet You at the Flagpole

Session Goals

This session's reading, reflection, discussion, and prayer will help participants:

- Reflect on the ways different people's perspectives, personalities, and passions lead to different interpretations of the world.
- Identify several basic distinctions of subject matter focus and style among Matthew, Mark, Luke, and John.
- Think about the nature of "passion" in their lives, and why the term is the traditional name for Jesus's arrest, suffering, and death.
- Compare and contrast the story of Jesus's prayer before his arrest in Matthew, Mark, and Luke, discovering how each Gospel writer emphasizes different aspects of the event's significance.
- Begin charting their personal faith journeys, looking for moments of special meaning that have shaped their relationship with God.

BIBLICAL FOUNDATIONS

They went to a place called Gethsemane, and [Jesus] said to his disciples, "Sit here while I pray." He took with him Peter and James and John and began to be distressed and agitated. And he said to them, "My soul is deeply grieved, even to death; remain here, and keep awake." And going a little farther, he threw himself on the ground and prayed that, if it were possible, the hour might pass from him. He said, "Abba, Father, for you all things are possible; remove this cup from me, yet not what I want but what you want." He came and found them sleeping, and he said to Peter, "Simon, are you asleep? Could you not keep awake one hour? Keep awake and pray that you may not come into the time of trial; the spirit indeed is willing, but the flesh is weak." And again he went away and prayed, saying the same words. And once more he came and found them sleeping, for their eyes were very heavy, and they did not know what to say to him. He came a third time and said to them, "Are you still sleeping and taking your rest? Enough! The hour has come; the Son of Man is betrayed into the hands of sinners. Get up, let us be going. Look, my betrayer is at hand."

Mark 14:32-42

Then Jesus went with them to a place called Gethsemane, and he said to his disciples, "Sit here while I go over there and pray." He took with him Peter and the two sons of Zebedee and began to be grieved and agitated. Then he said to them, "My soul is deeply grieved, even to death; remain here, and stay awake with me." And going a little farther, he threw himself on the ground and prayed, "My Father, if it is possible, let this cup pass from me, yet not what I want but what you want." Then he came to the disciples and found them sleeping, and he said to Peter, "So, could you not stay awake with me one hour? Stay awake and pray that you may not come into the time of trial; the spirit indeed is willing, but the flesh is weak." Again he went away for the second time and prayed, "My Father, if this cannot pass unless I drink it, your will be done." Again he came and found them sleeping, for their eyes were heavy. So leaving them again, he went away and prayed for the third time, saying the same words. Then he came to the disciples and said to them, "Are you still sleeping and taking your rest? Now the hour is at hand, and the Son of Man is betrayed into the hands of sinners. Get up, let us be going. Look, my betrayer is at hand."

Matthew 26:36-46

[Jesus] came out and went, as was his custom, to the Mount of Olives, and the disciples followed him. When he reached the place, he said to them, "Pray that you may not come into the time of trial." Then he withdrew from them about a stone's throw, knelt down, and prayed, "Father, if you are willing, remove this cup from me, yet not my will but yours be done." [[Then an angel from heaven appeared to him and gave him strength. In his anguish he prayed more earnestly, and his sweat became like great drops of blood falling down on the ground.]] When he got up from prayer, he came to the disciples and found them sleeping because of grief, and he said to them, "Why are you sleeping? Get up and pray that you may not come into the time of trial."

Luke 22:39-46

BEFORE YOUR SESSION

- Carefully and prayerfully read this session's Biblical Foundations, more than once. Note words and phrases that attract your attention and meditate on them. Make special note of how these Gospel stories are the same and different. Write down questions you have, and try to answer them, consulting trusted Bible commentaries.
- Carefully read the introduction and chapter 1 of *The Final Days* more than once.

- *You will need*: Bibles for in-person participants and/or screen slides prepared with Scripture texts for sharing (identify the translation used); newsprint or a markerboard and markers (for in-person sessions); paper, pens or pencils (in-person).
- If using the DVD or streaming video, preview the session 1 video segment. Choose the best time in your session plan for viewing it.

Starting Your Session

Welcome participants. Tell them why you are excited to study *The Final Days* with them. Invite them to speak briefly about why they are interested in this study and what they hope to gain from it.

Ask participants:

- When was a time—in your family, congregation, and/or your community—when you've heard or said such comments as, "That's not how it happened," "I don't remember it that way," or "You're telling it wrong!"?
- What factors can account for differences in the way different people experience and relate the same event?
- Have you ever deliberately changed how you tell a true-life story because of the way others tell their story of the same event, or for some other reason?
- Can multiple accounts of the same event all be true? Why or why not?

Tell participants the group will hear three accounts of Jesus's trial. Recruit three volunteers with Bibles. Instruct one to locate and read aloud Mark 14:61-62; the second, Matthew 26:63-64; and the third, Luke 22:67-71. After all three readings, ask:

- How does Jesus answer the question of whether he is the Messiah in each account?

- How, exactly, is this question phrased in each?
- Who asks this question of Jesus in each?
- What might account for the differences between these three accounts?
- Do differences and discrepancies among biblical accounts of the same event interest you? confuse you? trouble you? Why?

Tell participants Matt's investigation of the differences in the Gospels' accounts of this question to Jesus became an important turning point in his faith. Summarize his experience with the fellow Christians he met at the flagpole while in school, and their reaction to his questions about the Gospels' different perspectives. Note how these differences sparked for him a deeper inquiry into the nature of biblical narratives and the ways they inform our understanding of truth and faith. In *The Final Days*, Matt invites readers to undertake a similar investigation of discovery.

OPENING PRAYER

God of all knowledge, wisdom, and truth: In your grace, you have always sent your Spirit to stir the minds and hearts of many faithful servants to bear written witness to your great works. Pour out your Spirit upon us now, we pray, that as we read, discuss, and meditate on the writings of your servants Matthew, Mark, Luke, and John, we may encounter the Savior to whom they point us in new, refreshing, and challenging ways, deepening our faith and increasing our faithfulness; for we ask in the strong name of Jesus Christ, your Son, our Savior. Amen.

WATCH SESSION VIDEO

Watch the session 1 video segment together. Discuss:

- Which of Matt's statements most interested, intrigued, surprised, or confused you? Why?
- What questions does this video segment raise for you?

Witnessing through Filters and Lenses

Matt reflects on how his four children's different perspectives, personalities, and passions shape the way they interpret the world. Invite volunteers to speak briefly about how different people in their families (defined biologically or otherwise) interpret the world in different ways, and why. End this section of discussion by telling participants Matt suggests we can see a similar dynamic among the authors of the four New Testament Gospels.

Summarize some of the key characteristics of each Gospel as Matt describes them:

- Matthew–methodically presents Jesus's story as parallel to and fulfilling the Torah (specifically the Law given to Moses, and also, more generally, the first five Old Testament books); formal in language; useful for teaching.
- Mark–fast-paced; open to "mystery and unanswered questions"; presents a "terse" Jesus "less concerned about rules than he is about revealing salvation."
- Luke–presents a more expansive view of Jesus's identity and mission, extending Jesus's story to include the life of the early church in the Acts of the Apostles; pays special attention to the inclusion of "outcasts."
- John–special focus on Jesus's conversations with others; elegant language; treats time as a more theological than chronological category.

Invite volunteers to respond to Matt's descriptions of the Gospel writers, and to supplement his observations with any of their own. Ask:

- Do any of Matt's statements about differences among the Gospel writers' subject matter, focuses, and style surprise or confuse you? If so, which ones, and why? If not, why not?

- Do you have a favorite Gospel? a least favorite? Why or why not?
- Why does the church read four Gospels rather than simply read one?

FINDING YOUR PASSION

Ask:

- What are the different ways people use the word passion in everyday conversation?
- Matt defines passion as "something for which you are willing to suffer." Have you found such a passion in your life? If so, what is it? How did you discover it? How has it shaped your life?
- If you have not found such a passion, why do you think you haven't? What, if anything, are you doing to seek such a passion?
- Is it possible, or desirable, for passions to change throughout life? Why or why not?
- The story of Jesus's arrest, suffering, and death is traditionally called the story of his "Passion" (from the Latin *passio*, "suffering"). Do you think this is still a helpful and meaningful name for the story? Why or why not?

Tell participants the story of Jesus's passion begins after his last supper with his disciples, a story each Gospel writer tells in a different way. Your group will now explore three of the four tellings.

Form three small groups. Assign one group to read and discuss Mark 14:32-42; another group, Matthew 26:36-46; and the third group, Luke 22:39-46. (If meeting in person, have the small groups use different corners of your meeting space; if meeting virtually or in a hybrid setting, use your videoconferencing platform's breakout room capability.) Ask each group to answer these questions using their assigned Scripture. You may want to write these questions on newsprint or markerboard, or distribute them for ease of reference:

- Where do Jesus and his disciples go after the meal?

- What instructions does Jesus give his disciples when they arrive there?
- What does Jesus call God when he prays?
- How many times in this story does Jesus pray?
- What happens when Jesus prays?
- How would you describe the mood of this Scripture?
- What does this Scripture seem to emphasize most about Jesus's passion?

After allowing sufficient time for small group discussion, reconvene the whole group and ask for a "reporter" to share insights from each small group's discussion.

Point out ways in which the small groups' answers to the questions differ based on the assigned Scripture. Ask:

- Which of these differences, if any, seem minor to you? Which, if any, seem more important, and why?
- Matt says Mark's story emphasizes both Jesus's distress and his intimate approach to God, whom he calls "Abba" ("Daddy," "Papa"). When, if ever, have you experienced raw and anguished suffering? How, if at all, did that suffering affect your approach to God?
- Matt says Matthew's story emphasizes the purpose of Jesus's suffering. Have you ever identified a greater purpose in your own suffering? in the suffering of others? How?
- Matt says Luke's story emphasizes the anxiety and grief in the situation. When has "everything happened too fast" for you to process your suffering? What did you do?

What new insights, if any does examining these three Gospels' accounts of Jesus's prayer individually give you into the event and its significance for you?

Note: If you are leading a smaller group, discuss each of the Scriptures in turn with the whole group.

CLOSING YOUR SESSION

In his introduction to *The Final Days*, Matt tells readers they will read many stories about his personal faith journey and family life. His story about the prayer group at the flagpole and the service club with which he was involved are two such stories. "These anecdotes," he writes, "are not just personal reflections; they are windows into the broader themes of the book, inviting you to reflect on your own journey and the ways your faith is shaped by those around you."

Distribute paper and pens or pencils. Invite participants to draw a timeline and to mark points that represent moments they believe were important to their personal relationship with God or Jesus. Participants can also write the names of people who have been influential in their faith. After allowing sufficient time, invite any volunteers who wish to talk about one important moment or name from their timeline. Encourage participants to keep their timelines and to add to them as the group's study continues in future sessions.

CLOSING PRAYER

Lord Jesus, before your arrest and suffering, you prayed alone, as your disciples slept. May your Spirit keep us awake, willing to suffer with those who suffer even as we are willing to rejoice with those who rejoice, that in this Lenten season we may grow in love for you and for others, as you have first loved us. Amen.

Session 2
Looking for a Messiah

Session Goals

This session's reading, reflection, discussion, and prayer will help participants:

- Reflect on their experiences of unmet expectations, in stories and in their lives.
- Identify three prominent images for anointed messiah in the Old Testament and describe how each contributed to expectations for a messianic savior and can be applied to Jesus.
- Explore how Jesus both "followed the script" of messianic expectations and "rewrote the script" when he entered Jerusalem on Palm Sunday, as narrated by Matthew and Luke.
- Understand (in broad outline) three models of the atonement, and how they can help Christians make sense of Jesus's saving death on the cross.
- Meditate about areas in their life in which they need a Savior today.

BIBLICAL FOUNDATIONS

When [Jesus] had come near Bethphage and Bethany, at the place called the Mount of Olives, he sent two of the disciples, saying, "Go into the village ahead of you, and as you enter it you will find tied there a colt that has never been ridden. Untie it and bring it here. If anyone asks you, 'Why are you untying it?' just say this, 'The Lord needs it.'" So those who were sent departed and found it as he had told them. As they were untying the colt, its owners asked them, "Why are you untying the colt?" They said, "The Lord needs it." Then they brought it to Jesus, and after throwing their cloaks on the colt, they set Jesus on it. As he rode along, people kept spreading their cloaks on the road. Now as he was approaching the path down from the Mount of Olives, the whole multitude of the disciples began to praise God joyfully with a loud voice for all the deeds of power that they had seen, saying,

"Blessed is the king
who comes in the name of the Lord!
Peace in heaven,
and glory in the highest heaven!"

Luke 19:29-38

Then Jesus entered the temple and drove out all who were selling and buying in the temple, and he overturned the tables of the money changers and the seats of those who sold doves. He said to them, "It is written,

'My house shall be called a house of prayer,'
but you are making it a den of robbers."

The blind and the lame came to him in the temple, and he cured them. But when the chief priests and the scribes saw the amazing things that he did and heard the children crying out in the temple and saying, "Hosanna to the Son of David," they became angry and said to him, "Do you hear what these are saying?" Jesus said to them, "Yes; have you never read,

'Out of the mouths of infants and nursing babies
you have prepared praise for yourself'?"

Matthew 21:12-16

Before Your Session

- Carefully and prayerfully read this session's Biblical Foundations, more than once. Note words and phrases that attract your attention and meditate on them. Make special note of how these Gospel stories are the same and different. Write down questions you have, and try to answer them, consulting trusted Bible commentaries.
- Carefully read chapter 2 of *The Final Days*, more than once.
- You will need: Bibles for in-person participants and/or screen slides prepared with Scripture texts for sharing (identify the translation used); newsprint or a markerboard and markers (for in-person sessions); paper, pens or pencils (in-person).
- If using the DVD or streaming video, preview the session 2 video segment. Choose the best time in your session plan for viewing it.
- Optional: recorded instrumental music fitting for reflective meditation

Starting Your Session

Welcome participants. Ask for a few volunteers to tell a joke (keep it clean!). (Prepare a joke to tell yourself in order to "prime the pump.") Invite participants to talk about what makes a good joke work. Suggest, as Matt does, that good jokes work, in part, because they give those who hear them reliable clues about what to expect.

Ask:

- What kinds of stories, other than jokes, start by giving their audiences clues or signals about what to expect? (For example, Matt mentions fairy tales that begin, "Once upon a time," and *Star Wars* movies that begin, "A long time ago, in a galaxy far, far away.")
- Why do some stories fail to meet the expectations they create in their audiences? What happens when they do?
- How do we know when our expectations of a story need adjustment?
- When else in your life (other than in stories) have you experienced unmet expectations? What caused the gap between expectations and reality?

Tell participants that, in this session, your group will explore how and why the Gospels agree and disagree about expectations of a messiah, how some ways they present Jesus both meeting and not meeting those expectations of a messiah, and what those expectations may mean for Christians today.

OPENING PRAYER

Ancient of Days, you have always called and challenged your people to expect your mighty acts of deliverance. May your Spirit again summon us to look to you in hope during this time together. Free us from any expectations, or lack of them, that would dare limit your freedom to be the God who saves us, for we pray in the strong and saving name of Jesus Christ. Amen.

WATCH SESSION VIDEO

Watch the session 2 video segment together. Discuss:

- Which of Matt's statements most interested, intrigued, surprised, or confused you? Why?

- What questions does this video segment raise for you?

What It Means to Be Messiah

Read aloud from *The Final Days*: "The Hebrew Scriptures are far more than a Jesus prologue, but it is important to understand that without knowing the Scriptures Jesus and his contemporaries knew, it is easy to misunderstand or misrepresent the Gospel or more specifically the Passion accounts."

Tell participants, as Matt does in chapter 2 of his book, that the Hebrew word messiah means "anointed." Jesus and his fellow first-century Jews did not all hold the same expectations for a future messiah to come, any more than do all Jewish people today. As Matt states, "The Gospels don't offer a singular messianic hope."

The Hebrew Scriptures (Jewish Tanakh; Christian Old Testament) present three anointed, and thus messianic, offices: priest, king, and prophet. Recruit volunteers to find in their Bible and read aloud: the first to find and read Leviticus 8:10-12; a second to find and read 1 Samuel 16:6-13; and a third, 1 Kings 19:15-16, 19. After each Scripture reading, ask:

- What does the anointing in this Scripture symbolize or accomplish?
- Why does a priest (or prophet or king) need to be anointed?
- What ceremonies or rituals today, in church and/or in society, serve a similar purpose as anointing with oil did in the Old Testament?

Tell participants that, according to Matt, the three Gospels that narrate Jesus's institution of the Lord's Supper (Holy Communion) emphasize different aspects of Jesus's messiahship. Recruit volunteers to read aloud, one after the other, Mark 14:22-24 (almost certainly the earliest of the three accounts), Matthew 26:26-28, and Luke 22:19-21. Encourage other participants to read along silently. Ask:

- What similarities and differences among the accounts of Jesus's words do you notice?
- Matt says Matthew's account emphasizes Jesus as a priestly messiah. How so? Do you agree? Why or why not?
- Matt says Luke's account emphasizes Jesus as a prophetic messiah. How so? Do you agree? Why or why not?
- Which (if any) of the three messianic, anointed images—priest, king, or prophet—most closely matches your expectations or experience of Jesus as Messiah? How so?
- How helpful or unhelpful do you think these three images are for communicating belief in Jesus as Messiah in today's world, and why?

FOLLOW THE SCRIPT

Matt states that Jesus's entrance into Jerusalem on the day Christians now mark as Palm Sunday was Jesus's "very public announcement" of his messiahship. Recruit volunteers to read aloud the version of these events found in Luke 19:29-38, taking the roles of the narrator, Jesus, his disciples (verses 34, 38), and the colt's owners (verse 33). Discuss:

- Read Zechariah 9:9-10. What "script" does Zechariah's prophecy outline for a future king of God's people?
- How does Jesus's entrance into Jerusalem "follow the script" in Zechariah 9? How does it challenge other messianic expectations, both then and now?
- What does Jesus giving his disciples a "script" to follow when interacting with the colt's owners (verses 29-34) show readers about him?
- What does the disciples' acclamation of Jesus (verse 38) reveal about their expectations of his messiahship? Compare and contrast: Mark 11:9; Matthew 21:9; John 12:13. Who makes each of these acclamations? What significance do you find in the similarities and differences among them?

- Matt suggests Psalm 137 (a hymn composed during the nation of Judah's exile in Babylon) offers insights into people's expectations for a messiah. How so? Do you think people today want leaders who will deliver "payback" against their enemies? Why or why not?
- How does Matt say Jesus "rewrote the script"—in other words, did not follow the messianic "script"—after riding into Jerusalem?

Recruit a volunteer to read Matthew 21:12-16. Discuss:

- What is "surprising and scandalous," according to Matt, about Jesus's action in the Temple?
- Read Isaiah 56:1-8. What does Isaiah's prophecy communicate about God's character and purpose? Why does Jesus quote this passage (verse 13)?
- Matt says Jesus's prophetic action in the Temple "made room for those who needed God the most.... by driving away those who made worship a commodity." When, if ever, do you see Christians "commodifying" worship today—overtly or subtly, knowingly or unknowingly—and excluding those who urgently need God? How does your congregation avoid "commodifying" worship?
- What does it mean for God to prepare praise out of infants' and babies' mouths (verse 16; see Psalm 8)? Why does such praise anger these religious leaders? Do you believe God prepares praise from infants and babes today? If so, how? If not, why not?
- Matt says unmet expectations for God are a temptation to "let go" of faith. Do you agree? Why or why not? What do you tend to do when God doesn't meet your expectations?
- How does Matt say Luke connects Jesus's entry into Jerusalem with the three temptations Jesus experienced in the desert (Luke 4:1-12)?

MANY WAYS TO MAKE SENSE OF THE CROSS

Summarize Matt's experience preaching about different ways of understanding how Jesus's death on the cross saves. Tell participants that, historically, Christian theology has emphasized three "models of the atonement" to describe and explain how Jesus's death saves. The New Testament does not "teach" any one of these models; rather, all the models draw on some New Testament texts. These three models also do not exhaust New Testament ideas about and images for Jesus's saving death, but, over time, they have proven helpful to the church in thinking about how Jesus is Savior. As Matt discovered, the models can also reveal polarizing differences in Christians' expectations for the Messiah today.

Briefly present the three models, as Matt explains them:

- *Substitution Atonement Theory*: Jesus died in our place, taking upon himself the punishment our sin deserves, so we might have eternal life (see, for example, Romans 6:23).
- *Ransom Atonement Theory*: Jesus's suffering on the cross "pays the debt" for our sin so we can be regarded as righteous before God (see, for example, Mark 10:45).
- *Moral Exemplar Theory*: Jesus's death on the cross is the supreme example of how we are supposed to live and to die (see, for example, John 15:13).

Discuss:

- Which, if any, of these three models of the atonement is most familiar to you? Least familiar?
- What Scriptures can you think of or find (using a concordance or trusted online resources) to support each model? (Matt does not cite the biblical texts cited above, but groups could use them as starting points in their exploration.) What Scriptures about Jesus's death can you think of or find that do not clearly

support one of these models? (John 3:16 may be considered one of many such texts.)

- What questions, if any, do you think each of these models raise and leave unanswered? What problems, if any, do they present to how you think and what you believe about God and Jesus?
- How, if at all, do the models work together to convey a fuller understanding of how Jesus's death saves?
- Matt reports that some members left his church over his preaching of different models of the atonement. Why can "push[ing] against what someone assumes a messiah is to be" prove so "anxious and polarizing?"

Closing Your Session

Read aloud from *The Final Days*: "It's not that Jesus fulfills the [specific messianic] prophecies as much as offers a context that [both] helps us understand God's story and the future hope God's story proclaims."

Tell participants, as Matt does, that Lent is a time for telling the truth about ourselves. Ask them to reflect silently on these questions (you may wish to play instrumental music appropriate for meditation):

- What are some areas of your life in which you need a Savior to deliver you?
- What are the symptoms that let you recognize these areas of your life?
- What would deliverance look like for you?
- What is something you are doing or could do this Lent to make room for the coming Easter message of deliverance and resurrection?

Closing Prayer

Lord Jesus, though we can never fully understand how or all the ways in which you save, we believe that you do. May your Spirit continue to prepare us to experience the deliverance you bring and to live out of that liberating power in our relationship with you and with others. Amen.

Session 3

Yes, I Am: The Passion according to Mark

Session Goals

This session's readings, reflection, discussion, and prayer will help participants:

- Reflect on experiences of feeling like and being an "outsider" who fails to understand what "insiders" understand.
- Appreciate the Gospel of Mark's emphasis on the failure of Jesus's "insiders" to understand and believe in him.
- Identify literal and figurative "noise" in their lives that may be keeping them from clearly hearing Jesus and his Gospel, especially Jesus's connection of his messiahship to his cross.
- Consider how the details in Mark's account of Jesus's crucifixion paint an ironic picture of who correctly understands and responds to Jesus, and who does not.
- Think about ways to feed a holy imagination in response to Jesus's surprising resurrection.

Biblical Foundations

Jesus went on with his disciples to the villages of Caesarea Philippi, and on the way he asked his disciples, "Who do people say that I am?" And they answered him, "John the Baptist; and others, Elijah; and still others, one of the prophets." He asked them, "But who do you say that I am?" Peter answered him, "You are the Messiah." And he sternly ordered them not to tell anyone about him.

Then he began to teach them that the Son of Man must undergo great suffering and be rejected by the elders, the chief priests, and the scribes and be killed and after three days rise again. He said all this quite openly. And Peter took him aside and began to rebuke him. But turning and looking at his disciples, he rebuked Peter and said, "Get behind me, Satan! For you are setting your mind not on divine things but on human things."

Mark 8:27-33

It was nine o'clock in the morning when they crucified [Jesus]. The inscription of the charge against him read, "The King of the Jews." And with him they crucified two rebels, one on his right and one on his left. Those who passed by derided him, shaking their heads and saying, "Aha! You who would destroy the temple and build it in three days, save yourself, and come down from the cross!" In the same way the chief priests, along with the scribes, were also mocking him among themselves and saying, "He saved others; he cannot save himself. Let the Messiah, the King of Israel, come down from the cross now, so that we may see and believe." Those who were crucified with him also taunted him.

When it was noon, darkness came over the whole land until three in the afternoon. At three o'clock Jesus cried out with a loud voice, "Eloi, Eloi, lema sabachthani?" which means, "My God, my God, why have you forsaken me?" When some of the bystanders heard it, they said, "Listen, he is calling for Elijah." And someone ran, filled a sponge with sour wine, put it on a stick, and gave it to him to drink, saying, "Wait, let us see whether Elijah will come to take him down." Then Jesus gave a loud cry and breathed his last. And the curtain of the temple was torn in two, from top to bottom. Now when the centurion who stood facing him saw that in this way he breathed his last, he said, "Truly this man was God's Son!"

Mark 15:25-39

When the Sabbath was over, Mary Magdalene and Mary the mother of James and Salome bought spices, so that they might go and anoint him. And very early on the first day of the week, when the sun had risen, they went to the tomb. They had been saying to one another, "Who will roll away the stone for us from the entrance to the tomb?" When they looked up, they saw that the stone, which was very large, had already been rolled back. As they entered the tomb, they saw a young man dressed in a white robe sitting on the right side, and they were alarmed. But he said to them, "Do not be alarmed; you are looking for Jesus of Nazareth, who was crucified. He has been raised; he is not here. Look, there is the place they laid him. But go, tell his disciples and Peter that he is going ahead of you to Galilee; there you will see him, just as he told you." So they went out and fled from the tomb, for terror and amazement had seized them, and they said nothing to anyone, for they were afraid.

Mark 16:1-8

Before Your Session

- Carefully and prayerfully read this session's Biblical Foundations, more than once. Note words and phrases that attract your attention and meditate on them. Write down questions you have, and try to answer them, consulting trusted Bible commentaries.
- Carefully read chapter 3 of *The Final Days*, more than once.

- You will need: Bibles for in-person participants and/or screen slides prepared with Scripture texts for sharing (identify the translation used); newsprint or a markerboard and markers (for in-person sessions); paper, pens or pencils (in-person).
- If using the DVD or streaming video, preview the session 3 video segment. Choose the best time in your session plan for viewing it.

Starting Your Session

Welcome participants. Ask:

- When was a time you didn't understand something everyone else around you understood?
- How did this experience make you feel?
- If you were able to overcome your lack of understanding, how did you? If not, why not? What happened?
- When and how, if ever, have you helped someone who didn't understand something apparent to you and others around you?

Read aloud from *The Final Days*: "[The Gospel of Mark] makes more sense if you read it as a sermon to those already in [Jesus's] movement who are missing the point. . . . Throughout [Mark], those who are supposed to be on the inside didn't get it, and those who are supposed to be on the outside do."

Read aloud Mark 4:10-13, a passage Matt says is emblematic of Mark's emphasis on the comprehension of "insiders" and "outsiders." Ask:

- Why, according to this passage, does Jesus teach in parables?
- How does this stated reason for using parables confirm or challenge your ideas about parables? about Jesus?
- What do you do when you don't understand something about Jesus?

Tell participants that, in this session, your group will focus on how Mark's account of Jesus's passion highlights failures of Jesus's first followers to understand and believe in him, and how Jesus's followers today can both identity with and learn from those failures.

OPENING PRAYER

God Most High and Holy, in fierce and unrelenting love you draw near to your people and to the world. As we now read the written witness of your servant Mark, may we sense your presence and by your Spirit respond with urgency and joy to the good news of how you save in your Son, Jesus Christ. Amen.

WATCH SESSION VIDEO

Watch the session 3 video segment together. Discuss:

- Which of Matt's statements most interested, intrigued, surprised, or confused you? Why?
- What questions does this video segment raise for you?

TOO MUCH "NOISE" TO HEAR JESUS'S SECRET

Ask participants whether they agree with Matt's statement, "Sometimes life is too loud for things to make sense," and why they do or don't. Ask:

- What in your life right now is the "loudest," literally or otherwise, in demands for your attention and energy?
- How, if at all, have the "noise levels" in your life changed over time?
- How do you find or make quiet space and time to listen to yourself? to listen for Jesus?

Tell participants Matt suggests that Mark's Gospel illustrates how physical and spiritual "noise" can keep people from clearly hearing Jesus and his message.

Recruit volunteers to read aloud Mark 8:27-33, taking the roles of the narrator, Jesus, Peter, and other disciples (verse 28). Discuss:

- How do the disciples' various answers to Jesus's question (verses 27-28) reflect the "noise" surrounding Jesus and his message in Mark?
- What does Peter say about who Jesus is (verse 29)? What can we infer from verses 31-33 about what Peter meant by his statement?
- Why does Jesus forbid his disciples from revealing his "messianic secret" (verse 30)?
- What do people in society today, Christian and non-Christian alike, say about who Jesus is? Which of these responses, if any, do you find to be a "noisy" distraction from the truth about Jesus, and why?
- The "villages of Caesarea Philippi" (verse 27) were named for the Roman emperor, and the region had long been a worship center for several gods. How do political and religious "noise" keep us from hearing Jesus clearly today?
- "Jesus will announce that he is the Messiah," writes Matt, "but only in the shadow of the cross so the connection is clear." How would you state the connection between Jesus's messiahship and Jesus's cross? How does Mark 8:34-37 add to this discussion?
- Why does Matt say Peter's later denial of Jesus (Mark 14:66-72) are ironic statements of truth?
- Matt says we Christians are tempted "to lift the cross so high that we avoid the possibility of being nailed to it." When and how have you noticed this temptation in your own faith? What did you do, or what are you doing, about it?

THE CRUCIFIXION IN MARK

Invite participants to read to themselves Mark 15. Alternatively, recruit volunteers to read aloud Mark 15:25-39. Discuss:

- "The Crucifixion in Mark is loud and barbaric," Matt writes. What details do you notice that support this characterization? Why do you think Mark doesn't include what Matt calls the "sanitizing" details found in the other Gospels?
- How are the formal charges against Jesus that are posted over his head ironic (15:26)?
- Read Mark 10:32-45. How does Mark's account of those crucified with Jesus (15:27) echo the story in Mark 10? How does it clarify what Jesus calls his "baptism" and the definition of greatness he gives in Mark 10?
- The passersby "deride" or "blaspheme" Jesus (15:29). Why is this language of blasphemy ironic (see 14:63-64)? If blasphemy is, as Matt defines it, "to claim that what is wrong is right," where do you hear blasphemy in the world today? How might you be guilty of blasphemy?
- Matt tells the story of a young woman who experienced great disappointment and violated trust when her youth pastor let her and others down. Do you think the passersby are deriding or blaspheming Jesus out of a similar sense of violated trust? Why or why not? As Matt asks, how have you rebuilt your trust in others after someone has let you down?
- What is ironic about the religious leaders' mockery of Jesus (15:31-32)? What does "saving" seem to mean to them? How does the fact that Jesus does not save himself further recollect his teachings about greatness in Mark 10?
- Why do you think both of the rebels crucified with Jesus taunt him (15:32)? When have you experienced the human tendency to "pile on" when someone is suffering—and when have you been guilty of doing so yourself?

- Matt interprets the darkness in the hours before Jesus dies (15:33) as reflecting the crowd's "be[ing] blind to what is happening." Do you agree? What other or additional significance can you find in this darkness?
- How and why does the crowd at the cross misinterpret Jesus's only words from the cross in Mark (15:34)? How does what Jesus had taught earlier in Mark about Elijah's coming (9:11-13) deepen their misunderstanding?
- Matt suggests Jesus's question from the cross to God is also Mark's question to the church. How and where has the church, in history, abandoned Jesus? How and where is the church abandoning Jesus today? How does your congregation seek to ensure it does not abandon Jesus?
- Matt states the torn curtain in the Temple at Jesus's death (15:38) represents "no separation between the Holy of Holies and the rest of creation." What practical differences does this lack of separation make for religious insiders? for those outside religious communities? for society as a whole? for the natural world?
- What is the ironic significance of the centurion's proclamation about Jesus's identity in 15:39? How do his words relate to Peter's earlier proclamation about Jesus in the villages of Caesarea Philippi, and Jesus's teaching then about the cross?
- Why are women who closely followed Jesus during his life "looking on from a distance" (15:40-41) as he dies? Matt suggests the women stand back because they expect God to miraculously intervene. Have you ever expected a miraculous intervention? What happened? How did you respond?

Closing Your Session

Recruit a volunteer to read aloud Mark 16:1-8. Ask:

- Along with most biblical scholarship, Matt accepts verse 8 as the ending of Mark's Gospel. If it is, why do you think Mark ends his Gospel without any appearances of the risen Jesus?

- Matt says the women who came to Jesus's tomb were "expecting the wrong miracle"—God's rescue of Jesus from the cross—and so were surprised by the right one. Have you ever been surprised by God acting in one way when you expected God would act in another? What happened? How did you respond?
- Matt writes about the women's "holy imaginations [being] starved." What does it mean to have a holy imagination? How can and do Christians actively feed a holy imagination?
- According to Matt, Mark thinks the church "says a lot of nothing because [it] is afraid of what believing in the Resurrection might mean in the world." Do you agree? Why or why not? When, if ever, have you and/or your congregation been afraid to say and do what belief in the Resurrection called you to do and say? What will you say and do differently now?

CLOSING PRAYER

Risen and living Jesus, grant us the courage to praise you for causing problems and breaking the rules. Grant us the humility to thank you for stirring our souls and refusing to stay in your place. Grant us boldness to imagine new ways of taking up our cross to follow and serve you, for the good of our neighbors and to the glory of God. Amen.

Session 4

You Have Said So, but I Say to You—The Passion according to Matthew

Session Goals

This session's readings, reflection, discussion, and prayer will help participants:

- Recall times in their lives when they could or would not answer a question with a simple "yes" or "no," and apply insights from that experience to Caiaphas's question to Jesus in Matthew 26:63-64.
- Consider Jesus's answer to John's question about his identity in Matthew 11:2-6 in relation to their own questions about and for Jesus.
- Examine how Matthew's accounts of Peter, Judas, and Pilate during Jesus's passion highlight Matthew's special interest in Jesus dying for the forgiveness of sins.
- Hear and respond to Jesus's promise to be with his disciples despite their doubts.

- Identify examples of faith as right relationships rooted in God's love.

BIBLICAL FOUNDATIONS

When John heard in prison what the Messiah was doing, he sent word by his disciples and said to him, "Are you the one who is to come, or are we to wait for another?" Jesus answered them, "Go and tell John what you hear and see: the blind receive their sight, the lame walk, those with a skin disease are cleansed, the deaf hear, the dead are raised, and the poor have good news brought to them. And blessed is anyone who takes no offense at me."

Matthew 11:2-6

When Judas, [Jesus's] betrayer, saw that Jesus was condemned, he repented and brought back the thirty pieces of silver to the chief priests and the elders. He said, "I have sinned by betraying innocent blood." But they said, "What is that to us? See to it yourself." Throwing down the pieces of silver in the temple, he departed, and he went and hanged himself.

Matthew 27:3-5

Now at the festival the governor was accustomed to release a prisoner for the crowd, anyone whom they wanted. At that time they had a notorious prisoner called Jesus Barabbas. So after they had gathered, Pilate said to them, "Whom do you want me to release for you, Jesus Barabbas or Jesus who is called the Messiah?" For he realized that it was out of jealousy that they had handed him over. While he was sitting on the judgment seat, his wife sent word to him, "Have nothing to do with that innocent man, for today I have suffered a great deal because of a dream about him." Now the chief priests and the elders persuaded the crowds to ask for Barabbas and to have Jesus killed. The governor again said to them, "Which of the two do you want me to release for you?" And they said, "Barabbas." Pilate said to them, "Then what should I do with Jesus who is called the

Messiah?" All of them said, "Let him be crucified!" Then he asked, "Why, what evil has he done?" But they shouted all the more, "Let him be crucified!"

So when Pilate saw that he could do nothing but rather that a riot was beginning, he took some water and washed his hands before the crowd, saying, "I am innocent of this man's blood; see to it yourselves."

Matthew 27:15-24

Now the eleven disciples went to Galilee, to the mountain to which Jesus had directed them. When they saw him, they worshiped him, but they doubted. And Jesus came and said to them, "All authority in heaven and on earth has been given to me. Go therefore and make disciples of all nations, baptizing them in the name of the Father and of the Son and of the Holy Spirit and teaching them to obey everything that I have commanded you. And remember, I am with you always, to the end of the age."

Matthew 28:16-20

Before Your Session

- Carefully and prayerfully read this session's Biblical Foundations, more than once. Note words and phrases that attract your attention and meditate on them. Write down questions you have, and try to answer them, consulting trusted Bible commentaries.
- Carefully read chapter 4 of *The Final Days*, more than once.
- You will need: Bibles for in-person participants and/or screen slides prepared with Scripture texts for sharing (identify the translation used); newsprint or a markerboard and markers (for in-person sessions); paper, pens or pencils (in-person).
- If using the DVD or streaming video, preview the session 4 video segment. Choose the best time in your session plan for viewing it.

- *Note*: This session includes discussion of Judas's death by suicide. Be ready to provide support to participants who may be grieving a death by suicide or who struggle with suicidal ideation themselves. In the United States, the 988 Suicide & Crisis Lifeline (https://988lifeline.org/) provides free and confidential support and resources; other local resources may also be available in your area.

STARTING YOUR SESSION

Welcome participants. Ask volunteers to tell a story about a time in their life when they could or would not answer an important question with a simple "yes" or "no." Ask them what answer they gave, and why they gave it.

Tell participants that, for Matt, Caiaphas's question to Jesus, as the Gospel of Matthew relates it, is another such question. Read aloud Matthew 26:63-64. Remind participants, referring back to the discussion in session 1, that the differences among the Gospels in Jesus's answers to this question was an important turning point in Matt's faith, sparking his desire to understand each Gospel's unique perspective.

Ask:

- Why does Matt contend that for Jesus to answer "no" to Caiaphas's question would be incorrect, but so would be "accepting messiahship on Caiphas's terms"?
- How does Jesus's answer reframe Caiaphas's question?
- Compare Matthew 26:63-64 again to Mark 14:61-62. If you only had these two Scriptures, how might you characterize Mark and Matthew's different emphases and interests, as well as what convictions they shared?
- Can your own experiences of complicated questions help you relate to either Caiaphas or Jesus in this Scripture—or both? or neither? Why?

Tell participants this session will help your group see how Matthew's account of Jesus's passion highlights his distinctive interest in not only complicated questions but also the complicated issues of forgiveness and reconciliation.

Opening Prayer

God of the ages, you established an everlasting covenant with your people Israel, keeping it in an unexpectedly new way in your Son Jesus, who we joyfully call Emmanuel. May we know you as God powerfully with us in our study today, that we may understand more deeply, claim more fully, and extend to others more freely the forgiveness and grace you so lavishly pour out to us in Jesus, for we pray in his saving name. Amen.

Watch Session Video

Watch the session 4 video segment together. Discuss:

- Which of Matt's statements most interested, intrigued, surprised, or confused you? Why?
- What questions does this video segment raise for you?

Your Question Isn't Quite Right

Recruit volunteers to read aloud Matthew 11:2-6, taking the roles of the narrator, John's disciples, and Jesus. Discuss:

- When he baptized Jesus (Matthew 3:13-15), John seemed to believe Jesus was the one whose coming he had been proclaiming. Why do you think John now sends his disciples to ask Jesus about his identity?
- How and why does Jesus not give John's disciples a direct "yes" or "no" answer to John's question?
- Matt says that, like the question Caiaphas will ask Jesus, John's question to Jesus "isn't quite right." What might have been a better question for John to ask Jesus? How "right" do our questions have to be in order to ask them of Jesus?

- Have you ever wanted to ask Jesus, "Are you the one, or are we to wait for another?"
- Have you ever taken offense at Jesus? Have you known others who have? Why? How do you believe Jesus responds when people take offense at him?

FOR THE FORGIVENESS OF SINS

Tell participants Matt states that "being counted as righteous before God through Christ"—the atoning nature of Jesus's death—"is more important to Matthew" than to the other Gospels. He points to Jesus's words over the cup at the Last Supper (26:27b-28) as well as three stories within Matthew's Passion narrative to make his case, stating that Jesus's words over the cup are "less about doctrine, institution, or liturgy than . . . about prevenient grace in the face of denial, betrayal, and blasphemy."

Form three small groups. Assign each small group one of the following Scriptures to read and discuss:

- Matthew 26:69-75 (Peter denies Jesus)
- Matthew 27:3-10 (Judas repents and hangs himself)
- Matthew 27:15-26 (Pilate offers to release a prisoner)

Encourage each group to ask, in their discussions, how their assigned story points—positively or negatively, directly or indirectly—to the forgiveness available from God through Jesus. After allowing sufficient time for small group discussion, reconvene the whole group and ask for a "reporter" to share insights from each small group's discussion.

Discuss:

- As Matt points out, the other Gospels, after Jesus's resurrection, all specifically mention or feature Peter again (see Mark 16:7; Luke 24:34; John 21:15-19). Why doesn't Peter appear by name again in Matthew after he denies Jesus?

- What had Jesus earlier taught Peter about forgiveness in Matthew 18:21-22? How might this exchange help us understand Peter's apparent failure to seek forgiveness for denying Jesus? How might Peter have found hope in Jesus's teaching instead?
- Matt suggests Peter let his grief (26:75) "get the best of him" rather than "position himself for the possibility of reconciliation." Have you ever decided no reconciliation is possible after you have wronged someone or after someone has wronged you? How do or could you know whether you were correct? Would you make the same decision again? Why or why not?
- What do you think moves Judas to repent of having betrayed Jesus (27:3)? When, if ever, have you repented of something you've done after you saw its consequences?
- Why do these religious authorities reject Judas's confession of sin (27:4)? When in your own or another's experience have religious leaders rejected attempts at confession, repentance, and reconciliation?
- Read Exodus 21:32, which Matt suggests informs Judas's decision to hang himself. How so? When in your own or another's experience has a private interpretation of Scripture led to harm? How can reading Scripture with others help guard against dangerous interpretations of it?
- Do Jesus's words about his betrayer in Matthew 26:24 close off the possibility of repentance and forgiveness for Judas? Do you believe Jesus would have forgiven—or has forgiven—Judas? Why or why not?
- What is ironic about Pilate offering to release either Jesus "who is called the Messiah" or "Jesus Barabbas" ("Jesus, the son of the father") to the crowd (27:17)?
- Pilate claims no responsibility for Jesus's death (27:24), yet he is responsible for administering Roman justice in Judea, and his wife has warned him to have nothing to do with "that innocent man" (27:19). What motivates Pilate to declare his own

innocence? How do people in power today "wash their hands" of guilt? When and how have you?

- How is Pilate's behavior on his judgment seat, forgiving Barabbas and condemning Jesus, like and unlike the judgment and forgiveness of God?
- As Matt states, Matthew 27:25 is not "permission to blame the Jewish faith for eternity for Jesus's murder." Tragically, Christians have often read this verse in just that way. How can Christians today read and interpret this verse (and, indeed, the whole Passion story) without falling prey to the anti-Jewish prejudice and hatred that has characterized past interpretations?
- To which of the three men in these stories do you most relate: Peter, who did not attempt to seek forgiveness? Judas, who did not believe he could be forgiven? Pilate, who did not believe he needed forgiveness? Why?
- How do you understand the concept of forgiveness in your own life? What does it mean to you?"

Note: If you are leading a smaller group, discuss each of the Scriptures in turn with the whole group.

BUT SOME DOUBTED

Recruit a volunteer to read aloud Matthew 28:16-20. Discuss:

- What do you think "some" (NRSV) disciples doubted (compare NRSVue: "they doubted," without qualification) on the mountain with Jesus, and why?
- Matt tells the story of a family that felt angry at God. Are anger and doubt identical? Are they or can they be related? What other feelings do people feel as they "wrestle with the divine"?
- Read Psalm 13. Can you relate to the psalmist's movement from present sorrow and pain to future hope? Why or why not? How encouraging, if at all, do you think this psalm would be to someone who feels God's face is hidden?

- Commenting on Job 38-41, Matt writes, "God is taking Job on a tour of the universe because the only thing that can hold suffering at bay is beauty." Do you agree? Why or why not? When, if ever, has beholding beauty helped you through a time of sorrow and suffering?
- "Jesus's promise [to be with his disciples] doesn't depend on our faith." When and how, if ever, have you felt Jesus's presence despite your doubts? How has your congregation experienced Jesus's presence despite doubt, sorrow, or suffering?

Closing Your Session

Read aloud from *The Final Days*: The life of faith is "not about having all of the right answers, but…about right relationships rooted in God's love for us." Refer back to Matt's description of the Black Church Food Security Network (https://blackchurchfoodsecurity.net/) as one example of right relationships rooted in God's love, relationships that were sparked by "asking better questions."

Discuss:

- What specific examples can you point to, from your own or others' experience, of how asking better questions led to restoration, relationships, and new possibilities?
- How does your congregation actively and concretely encourage right relationships rooted in God's love?

Closing Prayer

Risen Christ, to whom all authority has been given: We praise you for your presence with us, despite our doubt, and thank you for the pardon you lovingly pour out upon us. Give us grace, by your Spirit, to pour out ourselves in love for each other and for the world, that we may sing to you with all our lives, rejoicing in your salvation. Amen.

Session 5

A New Covenant to Remember: The Passion according to Luke

Session Goals

This session's readings, reflection, discussion, and prayer will help participants:

- Reflect on special and memorable meals in their lives and connect those experiences to Jesus's meal with his disciples in Luke 22:14-23.
- Appreciate the fast pace of Luke's account of Jesus's passion, paying special attention to what and who Jesus takes time to remember during it.
- Examine the friendship Pilate and Herod forge during their shared opposition to Jesus, considering its implications for governmental and religious alliances today, and for their own ideas about their enemies.

- Ponder what Jesus's prayer for those who crucify him (23:43) and the petition of one of the men crucified with him (23:42) might teach Christians today about forgiving and being forgiven.
- Think about ways their congregation practices remembrance as a spiritual discipline.

Biblical Foundations

When [Jesus] got up from prayer, he came to the disciples and found them sleeping because of grief, and he said to them, "Why are you sleeping? Get up and pray that you may not come into the time of trial."

While he was still speaking, suddenly a crowd came, and the one called Judas, one of the twelve, was leading them. He approached Jesus to kiss him, but Jesus said to him, "Judas, is it with a kiss that you are betraying the Son of Man?" When those who were around him saw what was coming, they asked, "Lord, should we strike with the sword?" Then one of them struck the slave of the high priest and cut off his right ear. But Jesus said, "No more of this!" And he touched his ear and healed him.

Luke 22:45-51

When Pilate heard [the chief priests' charges against Jesus], he asked whether the man was a Galilean. And when he learned that he was under Herod's jurisdiction, he sent him off to Herod, who was himself in Jerusalem at that time. When Herod saw Jesus, he was very glad, for he had been wanting to see him for a long time because he had heard about him and was hoping to see him perform some sign. He questioned him at some length, but Jesus gave him no answer. The chief priests and the scribes stood by vehemently accusing him. Even Herod with his soldiers treated him with contempt and mocked him; then he put an elegant robe on him and sent him back to Pilate.

That same day Herod and Pilate became friends with each other; before this they had been enemies.

Luke 23:6-12

Two others also, who were criminals, were led away to be put to death with [Jesus]. When they came to the place that is called The Skull, they crucified Jesus there with the criminals, one on his right and one on his left. [[Then Jesus said, "Father, forgive them, for they do not know what they are doing."]]...

One of the criminals who were hanged there kept deriding him and saying, "Are you not the Messiah? Save yourself and us!" But the other rebuked him, saying, "Do you not fear God, since you are under the same sentence of condemnation? And we indeed have been condemned justly, for we are getting what we deserve for our deeds, but this man has done nothing wrong." Then he said, "Jesus, remember me when you come in your kingdom." He replied, "Truly I tell you, today you will be with me in paradise."

Luke 23:32-34a, 39-43

BEFORE YOUR SESSION

- Carefully and prayerfully read this session's Biblical Foundations, more than once. Note words and phrases that attract your attention and meditate on them. Write down questions you have, and try to answer them, consulting trusted Bible commentaries.
- Carefully read chapter 5 of *The Final Days*, more than once.
- You will need: Bibles for in-person participants and/or screen slides prepared with Scripture texts for sharing (identify the translation used); newsprint or a markerboard and markers (for in-person sessions); paper, pens or pencils (in-person).
- If using the DVD or streaming video, preview the session 5 video segment. Choose the best time in your session plan for viewing it.

Starting Your Session

Welcome participants. Ask and discuss:

- What is your favorite memory of a meal?
- What made that meal so memorable and special—the menu? the company? the time or location? the conversation around the table? something else?
- Do you have any special memories of celebrating Holy Communion (the Lord's Supper; the Eucharist)? If so, what made those occasions memorable?

Read aloud Luke 22:14-20. Ask:

- How does Jesus connect this Passover meal with his disciples to the "kingdom of God"?
- Unlike Mark or Matthew, Luke mentions two cups of wine in this Passover meal. What makes each of these cups significant?
- Also unlike Mark or Matthew, Luke says Jesus instructed his disciples to eat the bread "in remembrance of" him (compare 1 Corinthians 11:23-26). What does it mean to eat "in remembrance of" Jesus?
- What is a covenant? What does Jesus mean by speaking of a "new covenant" in his blood?

Tell participants that, in this session, your group will focus on what and who Jesus takes time to remember during his passion, according to Luke, and how Jesus's remembrances offer us insights into and instruction for following him.

Opening Prayer

Blessed are you, God our Savior, for remembering your holy covenant with your people, and keeping your promise of deliverance in Jesus Christ. Fill us with your Holy Spirit as we read and discuss the written witness of your servant Luke, that we may be strengthened and sustained to serve you without fear, trusting in your might and your mercy. Amen.

WATCH SESSION VIDEO

Watch the session 5 video segment together. Discuss:

- Which of Matt's statements most interested, intrigued, surprised, or confused you? Why?
- What questions does this video segment raise for you?

TAKING THE TIME TO PRAY AND HEAL

Recruit a volunteer to read aloud Luke 22:39-53. Discuss:

- As Matt notes, the "sense of urgency" in Luke's account of Jesus's passion is seen, among other details, in Jesus praying only once instead of three times (contrast Mark 14:35-41; Matthew 26:39-44)—yet Jesus still takes time to pray. How has taking or not taking time to pray in the midst of hurried, urgent circumstances shaped your experience of those situations?
- Although some ancient manuscripts of Luke do not include verses 43-44, they provide a vivid and memorable glimpse into Jesus's emotional life. When, if ever, have your prayers felt anguished? Have you felt angels, however you understand them, strengthening you in prayer? How?
- Luke says the disciples slept while Jesus prayed "because of grief" (verse 45). Why are the disciples grieving? When, if ever, have you known, as Matt calls it, "the lethargy of grief"? Why can grief exhaust us? What are some healthy ways to deal with grief's exhaustion?
- Has anyone ever called on you to "get up" in your grief, as Jesus calls on the disciples to do (verse 46)? Have you ever called on someone else to "get up" in their grief? What happened?
- Things happen fast in this account of Jesus's betrayal and arrest, but, unique to Luke's version, Jesus takes the time to heal the ear of the high priest's slave. What do you make of this detail?

- When and how, if ever, has someone taken time in a fast-moving situation to act for your healing and wholeness? When, if ever, have you done so for someone else?

Herod and Pilate

Recruit a volunteer to read aloud Luke 23:6-12. Discuss:

- Only Luke includes an account of Jesus appearing before Herod during his passion. Why does Luke say Pilate sent Jesus to Herod? Why does Luke say Herod was glad to see Jesus?
- Why do you think Jesus doesn't answer any of Herod's questions? How is his silence related or unrelated to his answer to the council in 22:66-71?
- Read Luke 13:31-33. What is Jesus's attitude toward Herod? How might this attitude inform his silence before Herod? Why does he let his works speak for themselves about who he is?
- Have you ever known or known of people who express Herod-like curiosity about Jesus? How can we judge whether someone's curiosity about or interest in Jesus is sincere—and should we try?
- Why had Herod and Pilate been enemies? What causes them to become friends? Do you think their friendship rests on a solid foundation? Why or why not?
- Matt attributes Herod and Pilate's newfound friendship to their shared recognition that Jesus threatens "the whole system in which they find their power." How, if at all, have you seen unlikely alliances between political and religious authorities form out of a shared desire for power?
- "If I need an enemy to maintain my identity," writes Matt, "then I never really discover who I am." Have you ever defined yourself by your enemies? Has anyone ever defined themselves by defining you as their enemy?
- Why does Matt say that loving your enemies (Luke 6:27) and loving yourself are closely related realities? Do you agree?

Remembrance and Forgiveness

Recruit volunteers to read aloud Luke 23:32-43, taking various roles, including Jesus and the two men crucified with him. Discuss:

- Some ancient manuscripts of Luke lack Jesus's prayer in verse 34. How, if at all, would the significance of this story change if we knew no tradition about Jesus taking time and sparing some of his dying breath to pray for those who crucified him?
- As Matt points out, Jesus does not, himself, forgive those who crucify him; rather, he prays for God to forgive them. How important do you think this distinction is? How does it connect to Jesus's teaching about forgiveness in 17:3-4?
- Should Jesus's prayer in verse 34 be a model for Christians today? Why or why not?
- "Forgiveness does not erase pain," writes Matt, "but it does mean we are no longer controlled by it." Do you agree? Why or why not? What else do you think forgiveness does or does not mean, and does or does not look like?
- Only Luke recounts the conversation among Jesus and the two men crucified with him. Based on this session's discussion, why do you think Luke preserved this tradition?
- How does the second crucified man's petition to Jesus (verse 42) contrast with the disciples' disagreement over greatness at the Last Supper (22:24-27)? In your experience, who does the church more often sound like today—the disciples or the second crucified man? Why?
- Do you think the second man's prayer is a prayer for forgiveness? Do you think Jesus forgives the man? Why or why not?
- Why does Jesus promise the man he will be with him in paradise "today"? How have you and your congregation experienced Jesus's kingdom as both coming and already present?
- Matt wonders if Jesus is remembering the garden of Eden when he speaks to the man of paradise (from the Greek root word

for "garden"). How is humanity's life in Eden an image of how Jesus will remember us?

Closing Your Session

Read aloud from *The Final Days*: "For Luke, Jesus's mission is less about atonement and more about a reconciled community with God at its center. This [kind of community] would be impossible without this spiritual discipline of remembrance." Discuss:

- How do you respond to Matt's assertion that Luke is less concerned with how Jesus atones than with the kind of community Jesus creates?
- Beyond celebrating Holy Communion, how does your congregation practice remembrance as a spiritual discipline? What opportunities does it create for regularly remembering its story with God?
- How do you practice remembrance as a spiritual discipline in your own life? How has it affected your faith?
- "Remembrance is not the power of the mind but the power of the Holy Spirit to unite us with the person of Christ in his life, suffering, death, and resurrection." When has your congregation experienced this union with Christ most?

Closing Prayer

Remember us, Lord Jesus, when you come into your kingdom at the new beginning of all things, and even today, when you come among us in your Holy Spirit. Make us whole in your body, that we may be reconciled with each other, forgiving and forgiven, taking the time to heal and to love others, for your sake and in your name. Amen.

SESSION 6

A WORD THAT WEEPS: THE PASSION ACCORDING TO JOHN

SESSION GOALS

This session's readings, reflection, discussion, and prayer will help participants:

- Think about times they have seen situations from a high vantage point and compare that experience to the vantage point of John's Gospel and of Jesus within John's Gospel.
- Consider Jesus's washing of his disciples' feet as the embodied epitome of the Incarnation and as an illustration of Paul's teaching about Jesus's humility in Philippians 2:5-11.
- Examine part of Pilate's interrogation of Jesus for indications of how Jesus's understanding of power and truth differ from the world's understanding.
- Appreciate the elegance of John's Passion account as signifiers of the birth of Jesus's beloved community, the church.

- Reflect on their study of *The Final Days* and how it has influenced their faith.

Biblical Foundations

Now before the festival of the Passover, Jesus knew that his hour had come to depart from this world and go to the Father. Having loved his own who were in the world, he loved them to the end. The devil had already decided that Judas son of Simon Iscariot would betray Jesus. And during supper Jesus, knowing that the Father had given all things into his hands and that he had come from God and was going to God, got up from supper, took off his outer robe, and tied a towel around himself. Then he poured water into a basin and began to wash the disciples' feet and to wipe them with the towel that was tied around him. He came to Simon Peter, who said to him, "Lord, are you going to wash my feet?" Jesus answered, "You do not know now what I am doing, but later you will understand." Peter said to him, "You will never wash my feet." Jesus answered, "Unless I wash you, you have no share with me." Simon Peter said to him, "Lord, not my feet only but also my hands and my head!"...

After he had washed their feet, had put on his robe, and had reclined again, he said to them, "Do you know what I have done to you? You call me Teacher and Lord, and you are right, for that is what I am. So if I, your Lord and Teacher, have washed your feet, you also ought to wash one another's feet."

John 13:1-9, 12-14

Then Pilate entered the headquarters again, summoned Jesus, and asked him, "Are you the King of the Jews?" Jesus answered, "Do you ask this on your own, or did others tell you about me?" Pilate replied, "I am not a Jew, am I? Your own nation and the chief priests have handed you over to me. What have you done?" Jesus answered, "My kingdom does not belong to this world. If my kingdom belonged to this world, my followers would be fighting to keep me from being handed over to the Jews. But as it is, my kingdom is not from here." Pilate asked him, "So you are a king?" Jesus answered, "You say that I am a king. For this I was born, and for this I came into the world, to testify to the truth. Everyone who belongs to the truth listens to my voice." Pilate asked him, "What is truth?"...

[Pilate] said to the Jews, "Here is your King!" They cried out, "Away with him! Away with him! Crucify him!" Pilate asked them, "Shall I crucify your King?" The chief priests answered, "We have no king but Caesar."

John 18:33-38a; 19:14b-15

Meanwhile, standing near the cross of Jesus were his mother, and his mother's sister, Mary the wife of Clopas, and Mary Magdalene. When Jesus saw his mother and the disciple whom he loved standing beside her, he said to his mother, "Woman, here is your son." Then he said to the disciple, "Here is your mother." And from that hour the disciple took her into his own home....

But when they came to Jesus and saw that he was already dead, they did not break his legs. Instead, one of the soldiers pierced his side with a spear, and at once blood and water came out. (He who saw this has testified so that you also may believe. His testimony is true, and he knows that he tells the truth, so that you also may continue to believe.)

John 19:25b-27, 33-35

BEFORE YOUR SESSION

- Carefully and prayerfully read this session's Biblical Foundations, more than once. Note words and phrases that attract your attention and meditate on them. Write down questions you have, and try to answer them, consulting trusted Bible commentaries.

- Carefully read chapter 6 of *The Final Days*, more than once.
- You will need: Bibles for in-person participants and/or screen slides prepared with Scripture texts for sharing (identify the translation used); newsprint or a markerboard and markers (for in-person sessions); paper, pens or pencils (in-person).
- If using the DVD or streaming video, preview the session 6 video segment. Choose the best time in your session plan for viewing it.

Starting Your Session

Welcome participants. Discuss:

- What's the highest physical vantage point you've ever had on a situation? *(For example, looking on city streets from a skyscraper, flying in a plane, and so on.)*
- What did you see from your high vantage point that others couldn't see?
- What thoughts and feelings did your high vantage point inspire?

Tell participants that, in this final session of your study together, your group will focus on how the Gospel of John narrates Jesus's passion. Read aloud John 1:1-5, 14, 18. Tell participants that not only does John tell Jesus's story from a higher vantage point than do Matthew, Mark, and Luke, but also, as Matt writes, "Jesus has a different vantage point in John than in the other Gospels." Together, your group will consider what these high vantage points reveal that Jesus's followers today need to see.

Opening Prayer

O God, seated on high, you look far down on the heavens and the earth. In Jesus Christ, your Word became flesh and lived among us as one of us. By your Holy Spirit, who gives new birth, grant that this time of study may help us see your beloved world and your beloved community as you do, that we may more fully trust and more faithfully bear witness to your life-giving love. Amen.

Watch Session Video

Watch the session 6 video segment together. Discuss:

- Which of Matt's statements most interested, intrigued, surprised, or confused you? Why?
- What questions does this video segment raise for you?

Everything about Jesus We Need to Know

Recruit three volunteers to read aloud John 13:1-14, taking the roles of the narrator, Jesus, and Peter. Discuss:

- How does John tell this story from two vantage points? How do these two perspectives interact to give us a fuller picture of this story's significance?
- Why does Matt say Jesus's knowledge of "his hour" (verse 1) is "not so much that Jesus knew the future as much as Jesus knows us"? Do you agree? Why or why not?
- Why does John make no mention of Jesus sharing bread and wine with his disciples during their last meal before his crucifixion?
- Matt states that, in this story, "John is telling us almost everything we need to know about who Christ is." Imagine this story were the only story about Jesus the church had. What would we know about him? What would we believe about him? What would we do for him and for others in his name?
- Read Philippians 2:5-11, which Matt quotes while discussing the story in John 13. How does Jesus's washing his disciples' feet illustrate this Scripture (which may be an ancient Christian hymn Paul is quoting)? How does it illustrate John's assertion that, in Jesus, God's Word became flesh (John 1:14)?
- Why does Peter initially object to Jesus washing his feet?

Why does he change his mind so quickly and wholeheartedly?

- "Sometimes," Matt writes, "touch can communicate a healing you didn't know you needed." How is Jesus's washing his disciples' feet an example of such a touch? Have you ever experienced healing—physical, spiritual, relational, or otherwise—through touch? Has your touch ever brought such healing to someone else?
- Why does Jesus tell his disciples he has washed their feet? Does your congregation celebrate a foot washing service? Why or why not? In what other ways, if any, can Christians obey Jesus's command to "wash each other's feet"? What might we lose and/or gain by substituting other actions for foot washing?
- What opportunities, if any, does your worship provide for Jesus's followers to make physical contact, and why?

Belonging to the Truth

Recruit three volunteers to read aloud John 18:33-38, taking the roles of the narrator, Jesus, and Pilate. Discuss:

- Matt states that, of all the Gospels, John makes Pilate's political use of Jesus most clear. How is Pilate's political gamesmanship on display in this conversation with Jesus?
- Why does Jesus want to know the source of Pilate's question about Jesus's kingship (verse 34)? What difference might it make whether Pilate is asking because others have prompted him or of his own initiative?
- Why does Pilate insist he is "not a Jew" (verse 35)? What does his reaction to Jesus's remark suggest about Pilate's relationship to his Jewish subjects?
- What does Jesus mean when he says his kingdom "does not belong to this world" (verse 36)? How does his statement highlight differences between how the world understands power and how he understands it?

- What is the relationship between Jesus's voice and truth (verse 37)? How can and do people listen to Jesus's voice today? Can someone who doesn't listen to Jesus's voice belong to the truth? Why or why not?
- Matt says Pilate's famous question about truth (verse 38) "isn't about philosophy as much as it is about... how fickle truth can be to those who have power." How, if ever, have you seen those in power treat truth as something fickle or manipulate truth for their own ends? When have you seen those in power take truth seriously?

Recruit two volunteers to read the words of the narrator and Pilate in 19:14b-15, while your group reads aloud in unison the words of the crowd. Discuss:

- John uses the phrase "the Jews" throughout his Gospel to identify people opposed to Jesus. How does framing Jesus's conflict as a conflict with "the Jews" obscure his and his followers' own Jewish identity? How has it contributed to antisemitic and anti-Jewish prejudice and violence throughout history? How should Christians read John's statements about "the Jews" today?
- How is Pilate's presentation of Jesus as the crowd's king ironic? How is it, as Matt points out, Pilate's "investment" in what he needs to represent Rome's authority over Judea?
- What is the irony in the crowd's acclamation of Caesar as their only king?
- How, if ever, do political authorities seek to manipulate God's people for their own ends, as Pilate did? How, if ever, does the church today fervently renounce its faith in God as its only ruler, Christ as its only lord?

Poetry in the Suffering

Recruit a volunteer to read aloud John 19:25b-27, 33-35. Discuss:

- Have you ever experienced someone's death as in any way elegant or beautiful? If so, how?
- Matt says John's account of Jesus's death has "almost an elegance" and is "horrifically beautiful." Do you agree? Why or why not?
- How does Jesus create a new family by presenting his mother and "the disciple whom he loved" to each other (verses 26-27)? How does Matt say Jesus's action represents his uniting those who follow him with God?
- How does the piercing of Jesus's side (verse 34) represent the sacraments of baptism and Holy Communion? Why does the narrator present testimony to this sight and emphasize the truthfulness of the one testifying?
- Read John 20:19-23. How and for what purpose does Jesus give his disciples the Holy Spirit after his resurrection? How does or how should the church forgive and retain sins today?
- Matt identifies the community, the sacraments, and the Spirit as the three essential elements of the church. How does or how should the pain involved in giving birth to the church shape its life today?

Closing Your Session

Read aloud from *The Final Days*: "Matthew, Mark, Luke, and John all offer their own unique pictures of Jesus's passion.... The narratives we weave from our encounters with the divine are as varied as the paths we walk. This diversity is not a flaw but a strength, inviting us to embrace the mystery and complexity of our spiritual lives.... In the end, our journey is about more than finding definitive answers; it's about engaging with the questions, experiencing the divine in our daily lives, and testifying to the transformative power of Christ."

Discuss:

- Which of the four Gospels' Passion narratives, as we have studied them, most resonates with you, and why? Which one most challenges you, and why?
- Which questions that we have engaged in our study will be ones you continue to think about and wrestle with, and why?
- How comfortable are you with the lack of definitive answers to some of your questions?
- Do you agree that diversity in the church's witness to Jesus and expression of faith is a strength? Why or why not?
- How will you testify to Christ's transformative power in your and your congregation's life as a result of this study?

Thank participants for studying *The Final Days* with you.

Closing Prayer

Lord Jesus Christ, you promise to draw all people and things to yourself. We thank you for this study we have shared and praise you for drawing us closer to you and to each other through it. May your Spirit continue to abide with and support us, that we may truly live as your beloved community, bearing witness to your power and love in many and joyful ways, that others may share our life with you and with our God. Amen.